Malaysia

Your Ultimate Guide to Travel, Culture, History, Food and More!

By Asha Miyazaki

Experience Everything Travel Guide Collection™

EXPERIENCE EVERYTHING
P U B L I S H I N G

Forward

Thank you for purchasing this book from the Experience Everything Travel Guide Collection™! Inside you will find a ton of useful, informative and entertaining information on Malaysia and it is our desire that this book will provide you with the inspiration to explore!

Disclaimer

While this book contains a great deal of information, it does not have all of the information that is available on the Internet. It is written to inspire you about the destination rather than act as a full travel guide that you could use to get from point A to point B or to specific addresses/locations during your tour.

CONTENTS:

Introduction

The tourism jingle of the country of Malaysia sings, "Malaysia, truly Asia". It has become a popular advertisement heard on radio and even seen on TV. You may wonder why and those who have been to the peninsula can give you this answer.

Peninsula Malaysia offers a diversified culture, history and friendly people. It has been a top choice among backpackers. It is also a popular destination for those who want to embark a trip to Southeast Asia. Aside from being a beautiful place, the country has a lot of tourist destinations to offer at a relatively cheaper price compared to its neighboring countries. You would be surprised that the country even has the cheapest rate for a 5-star hotel.

You can go shopping all you want for goodies to take home. The nightlife is also vibrant with crowds in the club including foreigners and locals. Beaches also surround the peninsula that would surely captivate your heart. Tourists often choose the pristine white sands of the Malaysian beaches because of its exclusivity. Apart from the refreshing, cool waters of the beaches, you can also take a dive in world-renowned coral-reefs. Rainforests, wildlife and national parks are also available for backpackers.

After you've finished going around cities and even in rural areas, give your famished stomach a treat with authentic Malayan dishes served in restaurants and even in hawker stalls along the streets. The rich flavors of the food in the country come with a distinct regional taste. Come on! Let's check out Malaysia through our travel guide.

Chapter I: Geography

Malaysia is located in Southeast Asia and shares a border with Thailand on its West. A bridge and a causeway connect the country to Singapore. It also has coastlines on the Malacca Strait and the South China Sea. On the east, the country shares borders with Indonesia and Brunei.

The country portrays the modern world with a touch of developing nation. Malaysia has moderate oil deposits and investments in modern technology industries. This made the country among the richer nations located in Southeast Asia. Visitors love to visit the country because of its happy mix of people, culture and high-tech infrastructure. You will also enjoy a less hectic lifestyle with prices remain more reasonable compared to that of Singapore.

The Malaysian Peninsula occupies territories between the countries of Singapore and Thailand. It is also the home of the most Malaysian population. The capital of the country is Kuala Lumpur. It is the biggest city and the most economically developed part of Malaysia. The West Coast of the country is also the most urbanized while the East Coast is more rural.

The eastern part of Malaysia holds rich and natural resources. It is also popular among visitors who seek tourism and industries. The Malaysian terrain is made up of mountains and plains in the coastal areas. It is separated by the mountain ranges called Barisan Titiwangsa. This mountain ranges runs from the Southern part of the country stretching to the North.

Experience the Company of the Malaysian People

The country is made up of a mixed society. The Malays make up the majority of the people in Malaysia. They hold a population of 52% while 27% of the population is dominated by the Chinese. You will also find Indians holding 9% and other races holding 13.5%. The indigenous people in Malaysia, the Orang Asli, hold 12% of the population in the country. This means that there is a fusion of religions including Christianity, Taoism, Hinduism, Islam, Buddhism and Sikhism. You will also find people practicing shamanism in the country.

Swaying Palm Trees and Raindrops

The country enjoys a tropical climate. From October to February, Borneo and the east coast experience the north-east monsoon. This causes heavy rain and flooding but the west coast is not greatly affected during this season. Meanwhile, from April to October, the south west monsoon affects regions in the country in reverse patterns. The southern part of the country, including the capital Kuala Lumpur, is also briefly yet intensely affected with rain showers.

Visitors who seek warm weather are guaranteed to feel it while touring the country. This is because the country is close to the equator. You will experience the scorching heat until noon when the temperature is at 32 degrees Celsius. By midnight, you will have a peaceful sleep with a cooler temperature of 26 degrees Celsius. Malaysia's sunny days are also interrupted with the Monsoon and experienced from November to February. Rainy days also bring a cooler temperature compared during summer seasons.

Meanwhile, the highlands in the country experience cooler weathers at around 17 degrees Celsius at night. At daytime, the highlands enjoy cooler days at 25 degrees Celsius. Those who are near or within Mount Kinabalu experiences temperatures that falls below 10 degrees Celsius.

Cities in Malaysia

Tourists who want to go around the cities of Malaysia will have a lot to choose from. You can start by visiting the multicultural city of Kuala Lumpur and get enthralled by the sight of the Petronas Towers. Get your stomachs famished by getting by the cuisine and cultural capital of Penang, George Town. If you happen to be in hype with history and colonial old towns, visiting Ipoh is a good choice. You can also drop by Johor Bahru which is also the gateway leading to nearby Singapore.

The commercial center of the east coast, Kuantan, is also a good destination for your shopping spree. If you want to experience nature at its finest, schedule a visit to Kota Kinabalu and its tropical islands. Those who want to take part of the colonial architecture can visit the historical city of Malacca. You can also drop by Kuching and Miri.

Spending in Malaysia

Like any other country, Malaysia also has its own currency. You have to make sure you have changed your money to ringgit. The Malaysian currency is abbreviated as MYR or RM. They also have coins which includes 5, 10, 20 and 50 sen. Coins are important as you will need these when you go to shopping malls, buying food from street vendors and in paying bus fares. However, some vendors may be hesitant to accept you 5 sen as this are only given as change in department stores.

You have to also make sure you ask the price you are quoted for especially when you are nearing the borders of Singapore or Brunei. This is because people refer to Singapore and Brunei dollars as ringgit as well. Travelers should remember that foreign currencies are not widely accepted in the country. Changing it to local currency is the best thing to do. This will save you time when doing your shopping or dining in a restaurant.

Visitors can also go to airports and banks to change their foreign currencies. You can do this if it's not urgent. However, you can always find licensed money changers inside major shopping stores. They often have good rates especially when you are changing big amounts. Be sure to ask for a quote regarding the exchange rate as this is often negotiable.

You can also get cash from ATM machines that are widely available within the city. If you are going on an island trip, bring only the cash you need as this might get lost or stolen along the way. Shops, restaurants and hotels also accept credit cards. However, you might encounter skimming problems when using your cards in smaller stores.

Chapter II: Malaysia History and Culture

The history of Malaysia has been regarded to be masked in mystery. It is also seen as a kind of black hole in history of Asian civilization. There is also not much archaeological evidence coming from the ancient civilization of the country. No written records have also been found. Many archaeologists think that there are more prehistoric sites inside the jungles or along the coastlines. However, the uncontrolled vegetation in the country will make it difficult to find ancient artifacts.

On the other hand, scientists have found homo sapiens were found in Malaysia a long time ago. The oldest known evidence of human inhabitation was found in a cave in Sarawak. A human skull was found in Niah Caves which can be traced back to 35,000 BC. There were also stone age tools that were found and were traced back to around 10,000 BC. Some archaeologists said that the tools could have been left by Negrito aborignes.

About 2,500 BC, a more advanced group of inhabitants from China moved to the peninsula. They were called the Proto-Malays who worked as farmers and seafarers. The new migrants were also responsible in sending the Negrito aborigens into the jungles and hills in the country. However, the cultural evolution in Malaysia has also created another group of settlers called the Deutero-Malays. These inhabitants included people coming from China, India, Siam, the Arabs and Proto-Malays. These people were known to have mastered the use of iron. Furthermore, these people also combined with Indonesians and have formed what we know today as the Malays.

The Golden Age of Malacca

The kingdoms of Indonesia and Cambodia have overshadowed the kingdoms of Malaysia until the 15th century. Records show that Indian, Arabs and Chinese peoples traded in the region of Srivijaya. The region was also regarded as the first maritime kingdom and other ports rivaled with the success of Srivijaya. However, the influence of the maritime kingdom declined after entrée ports emerged during the 13th century. Meanwhile, the strong central power and the nuisance of pirates have shaken the region.

The shaken maritime kingdom has caused the inception of Malacca in 1400 according to Malay Annals. This was established by Prince Parameswara of Palembang. The kingdom swiftly rose above other kingdoms when royal refugees inhabited the region. Malacca has also been regarded a perfect place for trading. It has been the most influential post in all of Southeast Asia for more than 50 years.

At one point during the golden age of Malacca, ships in all sizes can be seen in the harbor coming from different kingdoms. With trading happening in the ports of Malacca also came Islam. The rulers in the region have referred themselves as "sultans" who worked as the heads of an organized government in every municipality. Their main purpose was to make sure trading took place and that every coming ship was met by the harbor captain. The harbor captain would then ensure the needs of all vessels coming in to the port were provided. Aside from the thriving trade in the country and throughout Southeast Asia, Malacca was also able to take control even from pirates because of their alliances with the tribes. They have also outlined ports and established a navy police which escorted vessels who were in for trading.

Malacca has enjoyed its reign in the west coast of the peninsula. It has also control over a large area of Sumatra and the Pahang Kingdom. However, the region's success ended quickly as it was established with the Portuguese came to the country and took over. The colonial legacy left behind by the European invaders has influenced the country up to the 20th century.

Taking a Peek at the Colonial Times in Malaysia

The spice trade in the east first traversed through a route going to Egypt during the 16th century. Traders who were not Muslims were allowed to dock in the Arabian ports. Europeans were made aware of the fact that they needed another route for trading in the Far East and to India. Fearing they would be left behind, they decided to establish their own trading ports. By 1511, Alfonso de Albuquerque led the Portuguese fleet and conquered the city of Malacca. This also marked the end of the golden age of trade in the city.

A massive fort was established in Malacca by the Portuguese but was later on captured by the Dutch in 1641. This gave the Dutch an almost exclusive right to the spice trading but the British East India Company made efforts and convinced the Sultan of Kedah to allow them construct a fort in Penang in 1785.

The primary interest of the Brits was to make a safer route when traveling to China. However, the British rule in the region was amplified when France conquered Netherlands in 1795. The Dutch were in exile at the time and instead of handing the control of Malacca to the French, they agreed to let England temporarily look after the port in the area.

In 1808, the British returned Malacca to the Dutch but were later on returned to the Brits after a trade in Sumatra took place. In 1819, the Brits sent Sir William Raffles to establish a trading post in nearby country, Singapore. Penang, Malacca and Singapore then became the three colonies of the Brits known as the Straits Settlements.

Chapter III: Modes of Transportation

Most visitors who want to enter Malaysia are granted permits. You don't need a visa to be able to go around the country. Usually, these entry permits are granted on a 14, 30 or 90 days limit. You will get a visa stamped on your passport where the length of stay would also be specified. Members of the ASEAN countries can stay for up to 30 days in Malaysia without a visa except for Myanmar. After a month of stay, they will be required to secure a visa except for nationals from Singapore and Brunei. You have to ensure that you stay in the country within the allowable number of days indicated in your entry permits. Otherwise, you will have to a pay a fine valued about US$10 a day.

Plane Rides to Malaysia

There are a lot of transportation modes that you can choose from to enter Malaysia. The most popular choice among tourists is plane rides. Kuala Lumpur International Airport is the gateway of international visitors seeking to enter the country. Malaysia Airlines, the country's flag carrier, operates with a worldwide network coverage that reaches countries including Sri Lanka, Thailand, Vietnam, Philippines, Australia, China, Hong Kong, Laos, New Zealand, Cambodia, India, Thailand, Myanmar and Singapore, among others.

Aside from Malaysia Airlines, other budget carriers are also available including AirAsia and Malindo Air. Other airports in the country offer tourists rides going to local destinations such as Penang, Johor Bahru, Kota Kinabalu, Langkawi and Kuching. Airports in Malaysian cities mostly offer trips going to nearby Singapore. You can also take these rides going to Redang and Tioman where most diving spots are found.

Going to Malaysia by Train

Another mode of transportation that you can take is the train rides. The peninsula has railways that are operated by the Keretapi Tanah Melayu otherwise known as the Malayan Railways. You can go around the country using trains and can even travel to Thailand and Singapore. Train tickets can be purchase from online ticketing websites operated by KTM.

If you are planning to visit Malaysia from Thailand or the other way around, take the route operated by the State Railway of Thailand. This will give you access to Butterworth from Bangkok which is already near Penang. From Malaysia, you can go to Thailand by taking the KTM lines between Kuala Lumpur and Hat Yai, Thailand. Both lines cross the Padang Besar borders where immigration officials await those seeking to enter Malaysia and Thailand. Meanwhile, another route can be used although this is not a popular choice. The eastern route going to the Thai border, Sungai Kolok, can be taken from Hat Yai. However, there are no through trains that would take you to the nearest Malaysian station.

Meanwhile, you can also visit Malaysia from Singapore, vice versa. You can take the southern route of the KTM network. The lines have already been passing near the causeway at Woodlands Train Checkpoint in Singapore since July 1, 2011. You can take the overnight trains that connect Kuala Lumpur to Singapore. These trains also connect Tumpat and Kota Kinabalu. Take note that these train rides are priced with Singapore currency. That is why you have to carry enough Singaporean dollars because train rides going to Singapore from Malaysia or otherwise can cost twice as much compared to when you bought them in Malaysia.

Bus Rides in Malaysia

Travelers can also take buses from other countries going to Malaysia. These long-distance buses operate from Thailand, Borneo, Brunei and Singapore. Tourists coming from Brunei should take note that there are no direct rides from the country going to Malaysia. However, you can take the route from Miri and Limbang towards the border. From there you will be able to take bus rides going to Bandar Seri Begawan. Meanwhile, there are also direct bus rides from Indonesia. You can take them between West Kalimantan and Pontianak. You can also ride from Kuching in Sarawak going to Malaysia.

On the other hand, those coming in from Singapore can choose from a number of bus companies that operate directly to Malaysia. Various routes are offered making sure that you get to the right destination of your choice. Bus rides from Singapore can take you to Malacca, Penang, the East Coast and Kuala Lumpur. There are also routes going to the suburbs of Kuala Lumpur including Subang Jaya and Petaling Jaya.

Taking bus rides from Thailand is also possible when you want to go to Kuala Lumpur. Other routes from Thailand can take you to Hat Yai, vice versa. There are also other buses in Malaysia that will lead you to Bangkok and other Thai cities.

Long Drive to Malaysia

It is also possible that you enter Malaysia by car from Singapore or from the southern part of Thailand. You can also drive your way to the country from Kalimantan and Brunei going to Sarawak. You will need to have an International Drivers Permit to be able to drive going to Malaysia. Check out the information on driving indicated per respective city to ensure that you won't have to deal with road violations along the way.

From Malaysia, you can cross Sungai Tujoh going to the Bandar Seri Begawan. You can also cross the border going to Kuala Lurah Tedungan. Take the route from Limbang through Pandaruan as well as Lawas via Trusan.

Driving from Indonesia going to Malaysia is also possible by taking the crossing from Tebedu-Entikong checkpoint. You can also cross minor borders which are used by locals. However, be sure to ask if it can also be accessed by foreigners.

From Singapore, you can cross the Causeway connecting Woodlands and Johor Bahru. You can also take the Second Link connecting Tuas and Tanjung Kupang. Meanwhile, driving from Thailand to Malaysia is also possible with international checkpoints located in Wang Kelian, Perlis, Perak, Kelantan and Kedah.

Boat Rides Going to Malaysia

Aside from planes, buses, cars and trains, you can also take the boat to enter the country from neighboring places. There are ferries operating in Malaysia that are connected with southern part of Thailand, Indonesia, Brunei, East Kalimantan as well as Sabah. You can even enter the country through ferry rides from Mindanao, Philippines. There are also luxury cruises that operate from Singapore and Phuket going to Malaysia.

From Brunei, you can take boat rides on a daily basis found in Labuan Island at the Muara Ferry Terminal that will take you to Sarawak. You can also ride speedboats that operate mostly in the morning that would take you to Limbang, Sarawak. Boat rides going to Malaysia from Indonesia is also available. You will embark on a trip from the off points in Indonesia located in Riau Islands and Karimun. There are also other jumping-off points from Indonesia going to the peninsula. You can browse each of these from the internet or you may ask the local tourism office for detailed instructions.

Boat rides are also available from the Philippines going to Peninsula Malaysia. You can take a boat ride from Zamboanga that will take you to Sandakan, Sabah. Meanwhile, those who wish to take a ferry ride from Singapore can avail of tickets on daily basis. You can take a boat ride from Changi Point and Pengerang that will lead you to Johor.

On the other hand, there are four ferries operating daily in Thailand that would take you to Malaysia. You can take this should you wish to go to Tammalang or Langkawi, Malaysia. These ferries also operate near Tak Bai going to Kelantan. Meanwhile, there are also passenger boats operating from Ban Buketa going to Kelantan.

Walking Around Malaysia

Before, walking from Causeway, Singapore going to Malaysia was allowed. However, new mandates have declared getting to Malaysia by foot from Singapore to be illegal. On the other hand, you can still walk to and fro from Thailand to Malaysia.

Hail a Cab

Taxis are also abundant in Malaysia and another mode of public transportation available for both locals and foreigners. Bigger towns and cities in the peninsula have taxis operating that will take you to your next destination. However, if you are smaller places you will have to call for a cab. Numbers are usually found on the yellow pages of the directory or you may ask the front desk officer of the hotel where you are currently checked in.

Charges vary depending on the distance of the trip. Usually, you will be charged RM5 for a short distance trip. Meanwhile, you will be charged RM100 for a full day taxi rent. In Kuala Lumpur, you can spot a budget taxi through its color. Red, Yellow and White taxis operate in the city and are not allowed to go out of town. If you want to take a cab in going out of town, halt a blue taxi. These are bigger and more luxurious compared to the budget ones. The prices are also a lot expensive. You can find these taxis in major hotels and malls while the metered budget taxis can be hailed from off roads.

Before hoping aboard and enjoying a taxi ride, check first if the taxi driver is Malaysian or at least a PR holder. This is because some taxi operators rent their cabs to unlicensed drivers which can cause trouble once caught by traffic enforcers.

Tourists should also be aware of unlicensed taxis found in the airports. These taxis are dangerous because they can rob passengers from a single taxi ride. Authorized operators are found in the airport that are guaranteed to be safe and would charge you the right amount for the trip incurred. Metered taxis usually charged a flat rate of RM3 plus RM1 for every kilometer. Meanwhile, Blue taxis will cost RM6 plus RM2 for every kilometer.

Traffic Safety Measures in the Country

Malaysia ensures traffic safety for drivers. Like most countries, driving while under the influence of alcohol is a serious offense. If you are caught driving drunk, you will undergo a breathalyzer test conducted by a police officer. Once found guilty, never offer bribes as this can get you to spend 20 years in jail. Meanwhile, those who are crossing the streets should also be extra careful. Drivers usually disregard pedestrians which can get you bumped by a car. However, you can always ask for assistance from the Malaysian police who are very helpful. You can also dial 999 for assistance.

Chapter IV: Where to Stay While in Malaysia

There are a lot of places to go around Malaysia. The most important thing is to look around over the internet or ask your travel agent for great yet affordable places to book your stay. This will save you more time and the hassle of thinking and looking around for a hotel upon arrival. Usually, hotels get fully booked especially during holidays and travel season. If you have already booked ahead of schedule, you are sure to spend a comfortable and memorable vacation in the country.

Choosing Hotels While In Malaysia

There are a lot of hotel choices while in the country. Prices also range from the type of accommodation you choose and the location of the hotel where you plan to book your stay. Inexpensive roadhouses are also available while there are also five star hotels with luxurious amenities.

Facilities also differ with the kind of accommodation you choose. The basics include a box room with a bed while luxury hotels have business facilities, flat screen TVs, spas and private pools. There are also a lot of heritage hotels in the countries situated in colonial villas and even historic mansions.

If you are visiting Kuala Lumpur, don't worry because the city does not have hotel shortage. However, if you are planning to visit smaller cities, you need to make an advance booking especially during holidays. Visitors who plan a trip to Malaysia during the dry season should prepare their pockets because the prices reach at its peak. Cheaper prices are usually offered during the monsoon months.

Finding Resort Accommodation in the Country

There are numerous resorts in Malaysia that are best known all throughout Asia. Often, these resorts have their own pools and spas. Restaurants are also thriving that can be found just along the coast of the beaches. Activities are also flourishing including watersports as well as scuba diving. The prices for these resorts also vary.

Tourists can find resorts that are moderately priced especially during off season. Budget resorts can also be booked ahead for great discounts and affordable room rates.

Going Camping in Malaysia

You can also try camping when in Malaysia as there are numerous national parks and camping facilities. Tourists can also find wild camping sites along shorelines and in the other parts of the country. Meanwhile, you can rent tents, mosquito nets and beds in national park campsites. If you use your own equipment for camping, you have to seek permission from park authorities.

Other Accommodation While in Malaysia

Aside from hotels, there are also other accommodations that you can have your stay booked with. Cheaper ones such as the Youth Hostels is a good choice for both price and safety. Malaysia has been a member of the International Youth Hostel Federation, offering cheaper-priced youth hostels around the country. You will find these hostels in Malacca, Langkawi and in the capital city, Kuala Lumpur. Most of these hostels also offer set meals so you won't have difficulty cooking your food or looking for restaurants whenever you feel hungry.

Another type of lodging you can choose when in Malaysia is homestay accommodation. The government has allowed home staying through a program authorizing family homes in rural areas to accept guests. You will get the chance to experience a great atmosphere when you choose to stay in a tribal longhouse when you visit Borneo. However, you have to make prior arrangements as this type of accommodation has strict rules to follow.

Travelers who want to book a stay backpacker hostels can also make a prior booking. Malaysia is known to be a popular destination for backpackers making hostels and rest houses abundant all over the country. Most of these guest houses have internet, air conditioned rooms and lockers for your valuables. Take note that bathrooms are shared and noise can be a cause of discomfort as there are usually a lot of people taking this kind of accommodation while in Malaysia.

Booking for Mid-Range to Luxurious Hotels

There are a lot of mid-ranged hotels available about anywhere in the country. The price can start from RM100 for a 3 to 4 star hotel. You can be sure that these hotels will offer you quality service and rooms. Meanwhile, if you happen to have a lot of money and don't mind spending big on accommodation, you can always get a 5 star hotel room in cities like Penang, Kota Kinabalu, Kuala Lumpur, Johor Bahru and Kunching. Upscale accommodation can also be found in islands designed for affluent travelers. Although you are to book a 5-star accommodation, don't worry because Malaysia has been known to have the cheapest priced hotels in the world.

Malaysia would be on top of the list when it comes to diversity. Aside from being a melting pot of ethnic cultures, you will also experience different customs, religions and great foods. You will also feel safe as Christians and Muslims coexist peacefully in the country.

Vacations in Resorts and Beaches

Malaysia holds a number of beautiful resorts and beaches. Contrary to popular belief, booking a stay with resorts and beaches in an island while in Malaysia is not that expensive. For instance, you can spend a day or two at the Colorful Motel in Langkawi. You can see 104 tiny islands from a distance and can go for a dive in coral-reefs diving site. The motel offers basic accommodation but with private bathrooms and air condition. You can also expect a clean room throughout your stay. Just next to the motol is the Babylon bar and other famous nightspots in Cenang. You can book a stay for around RM120 a night for a double room accommodation.

If you happen to be in Langkawi, check out the Four Seasons Resort. Most travelers choose this destination because of the pristine beaches, white sand and marvelous limestone outcrops found by the edge of the water. If you want to see eccentric sights, you can also go to Scarborough where you will be served fish and chips while on the beach.

While in Batu Ferringhi, Penang, book a stay with Lone Pine Resort. Most tourists who have stayed with the resort admired the colonial buildings it has to offer along with vintage furniture and other old decorations covering the walls. Rooms are also spacious, bright and have a minimalist ambiance. You can also watch the sea from the balcony or relax on the seashore as this can be accessed few steps away from the resort. At night, you can enjoy partying with an in-house DJ as the entire Lone Pine's Batubar becomes lively with bars and clubs.

Accommodations at Chymes while Tanjung Bungah, Penang is also a good choice for travelers who seek exclusivity. You will be able to see luxurious condominums in this exclusive area with old houses elegantly tucked away along the roads.

While on the East Coast of Malaysia, check the Maznah Guest House in Cherating, Pahang. You will be able to enjoy the tropical beaches in this area that stretches up to 400 miles bordering Thailand to its north down to Singapore. There are also a lot of islands around the area which is ideal for scuba diving. Guests can stay in simple huts. Take note that toilets are shared and rooms are often equipped with fans only. However, you can take the modern bungalow accommodation should you wish to have an air conditioned room.

Chapter V: Where to Go and What to Eat

If you are planning to spend the holidays in Peninsula Malaysia, you can choose from a lot of tourist hot spots within the country. This will allow you to experience the Malaysian culture and the beauty of the entire country as well as its people. Aside from visiting tourist spots and getting enthralled from the different activities you can engage in, you can also feast on sumptuous Malaysian cuisine and get your stomachs delighted with tasty street foods.

Top 10 Destinations in Malaysia

Kota Bharu is best known to be a popular stopover place for most tourists who are heading to Perhentian Islands. Kota Bharu is located near the border of Thailand and offers tourists shopping, great food, attractions and a unique charm that would get you enchanted. You will also find cheap but quality items that you can bring home. The city is also easy to explore by taxi, a bus ride of even by walking.

You can also head to Melaka, the busy route most travelers take when going to China or India. It is located in the southwest coast of the country. The city has rich history after being in battle for centuries during the colonial era of the British, Portuguese, Indian and Dutch governments. As a result, the city displays a modern day Malaysian city with a touch of diversified cultures. Tourists will be able to check out great architecture and eat great cuisines all packed with various flavors.

Tourists can also visit Cameron Highlands for a cooler ambiance. This will give you ample time to refresh your senses from the hustle and bustle of the lowlands. The Cameron Highlands is located in Titiwangsa Mountains. It is also among the oldest tourist destination in the country offering visitors colorful flower farms, lush scenery and other outdoor recreation. You will also enjoy the views of lakes and forests as well as going around the tea plantation of the highlands.

Another fast growing tourist destination is the capital of Sabah, Kota Kinabalu. Tourists often visit the place because it is near islands, wildlife parks, rainforests and the country's tallest peak, Mount Kinabalu. You can also take a turn and visit the biggest city on the Borneo Island, Kuching. It is a popular destination in Sarawak because of its rainforests and historical landmarks. Tourists often enjoy spending their time on outdoor activities as well as shopping and exploring the city's busy markets.

Meanwhile, Penang Island has been attracting more and more visitors because of its cultural diversity and historic places. George Town can be found in this area along with great food and splendid architecture. The island is also the most traveled shipping route in the world. You can also head on to Kuala Lumpur, the country's capital, for nightlife, dining and shopping. You will find skyscrapers and modern-day living in KL, as most locals call it.

Don't forget to check out Taman Negara for great ecotourism activities. You will be able to see the Malayan Tiger and the Sumatran Rhinoceros along with exotic birds and the Asian elephant in this area. It also has national parks and holds the oldest rainforest in the world. Meanwhile, beach bums should visit Langkawi where about 99 islands are situated. Beautiful beach sceneries can be found in this area along with mangroves and rainforests. Visitors don't have to worry about spending their vacation in the area as more hotels and resorts have opened their doors to accommodate more people. Those who want to experience outdoor activities can visit the Gunung Mulu National Park. You will find a limestone karst formation in this area along with spectacular caves.

Food, Food and More Food!

Going around Malaysia will not be complete without having to taste the delicious cuisine of the country. Start off with the Apam balik, a sweet treat snack made with omelet and sugar. Sometimes, this is sprinkled with corn and peanuts. The Mee goreng mamak or yellow noodles is actually an Indian Muslim dish. It is made with shrimp, soy sauce, vegetable and eggs as well as beef or chicken. It is completed with a bit of chili for that best hot taste. This is best eaten in a hawker stall as it will never taste the same when you try to copy and cook it at home.

Another must try dish is the Nasi kerabu. You will get intrigued with this blue rice and colorful flowers mixed together to form the dish. This Kelantanese dish often gets people to line in numbers while waiting for their orders. The dish is completed with bean sprouts and fried coconut with spicy fish sauce.

Don't forget to try the Ayam percik. This is made with chicken in percik sauce and is available even in KFC food chains. The chicken is barbecued and is slathered with garlic, ginger and chili sauce. It is then mixed with coconut milk and just the right amount of percik sauce.

And then there's Roti John. No, this is not a person. It is still a Malaysian food made with sandwiches, egg, condiments and minced meat. You can choose to have it spicy, sweet or a combination of all flavors. For those who want a less oily snack, you can go for the popia basah. It is made with lettuce, turnips, bean sprouts and fried onions with a specific regional taste.

Aside from going to restaurants for Malaysian cuisine, you can also find food along the streets. Vendors are abundant along the streets that will offer you great tasting foods. A popular street food is the assam laksa found in Weld Quay in George Town. It is made with rice noodles with tamarind and drenched in fish soup. Another street food to try is the rojak. It is made with fruit and brown sauce and sometimes with fried squid or fried dough. The sauce has never been divulged making it a mystery for those who have tried it.

Hungry? Get a taste of the apom balik while on the streets. It is made from sticky rice flour with creamed corn inside. You will find this sold at Tan Jetty and is usually fluffy and eggy. You will enjoy every sticky bite along with its crisp edge. On the little lanes found in Lorong Baru, hawker stalls are selling Batu Maung satay. These are grilled pork, beef or chicken on skewers. They are served with white onions and cucumber or according to what you prefer.

There's a lot more to unravel when it comes to Malaysian cuisine. You can check out restaurants in the cities and in smaller areas to get a taste of authentic dishes. The streets are also the best places to scout for authentic

Malayan food. You can never go hungry when in Malaysia as foods are abundantly sold almost anywhere. The best thing about it? It costs cheap to get your stomachs full.

Chapter VI: Must See Festivals and Events

The amazing different cultures of Malaysia are one of the great events that you can experience with many festivals that mark the country's dates of events. The feasts that surround Malaysia will cater a big opportunity for you to witness the amazing ways in which many and different religions, cultures and traditions have blended gracefully, making this country's the most beautiful destination that attracts tourists every year.

Malaysia is a country of different and many cultures exercising many culture as well as different religions. Each ethnicity exercise has its own belief and religions which mean variety of festivals are celebrated the whole year. These festivals are always celebrated either nationwide or a state level. A concept practiced by many festivals is the "Open house", which means relatives and friends are invited to join and partake the food and festivity of the occasion. Some of these festivals are usually public holidays.

Holidays in Malaysia

Malaysia holds colorful and interesting festivals. Those who wish to visit the country can plan their vacations ahead to ensure they would be able to attend the festivities for the month. This will give you a better appreciation of the country, its culture along with its people.

If you plan to visit the country in January or February, you can witness the Chinese New Year celebration. Malaysians celebrate the lunar New Year in a grand manner. The Chinese communities found in the country adorn their houses with Chinese decors seeking good luck, money and good fortune. Streets and other establishments are also decorated with traditional adornments. During this time, families gather together and eat Chinese foods that symbolize life, energy and fortune.

Aside from the celebration of the Chinese New Year, the Hindus also have their own New Year festival. This is known as the Hindu Festival of Lights where very colorful lights symbolize hope and victory against evil and darkness. It also symbolizes overcoming the challenges confronting the

Hindus. This is celebrated in October or November, the same time when Hindu homes and temples also spend their time in prayers. On this day, the Hindus wake up early morning to bathe with oil before starting their prayers.

Meanwhile, Hindu temples are lighted with oil lamps with processions and fireworks following after. This also celebrated in communities where Indians are located such as Little India found in Kuala Lumpur. If you get lucky to be invited in this festival, you will get the chance to taste great Indian flavored foods.

Another important Muslim event in the country is the month of fasting, Ramadan. The Hari Raya Puasa marks the end of Ramadan. During this time, people celebrate with prayers and open their homes to fellow Muslims to share food. Muslim homes also share food with other people in the community. Tourists can also witness the best cuisine offered to Malay homes and their loved ones. The elderly give children monetary gifts placed in green packets.

Other Religious Festivals in Malaysia

Another Hindu festival celebrated in the country by the Tamil community starts from Sri Mahamarianman Temple. It starts in Kuala Lumpur going to Batu Caves. The procession last for eight hours and culminates by going up the top of the caves in a stairs composed of 272 steps. This attracts more than one million devotees and thousands of tourists that want to experience the culture. The devotees bring kavadis, sacrificial burdens, to seek help and blessings. Ipoh, Penang and Perak also have celebrations in other cave sites.

Buddhists also have their own celebration called the Wesak day. This is celebrated to remember the important days in the life of Buddha including his achievement of Nirvana, birthday and enlightenment. The start of the festival for Buddhists begins early at dawn. People start to gather to meditate. They also give food and endowments to the needy. They also offer incense and joss sticks and spend time in prayer.

The highlight of the celebration is the float parade where the statue of Buddha is featured.

Timeline of Festivals and Fiestas in Malaysia

Tourists will enjoy the celebration of festivals and fiestas in the country because of its significant characteristics. You will enjoy experiencing the Malaysian culture through its numerous celebrations all throughout the year. This is also the time when families get together and enjoy time together in celebrating the holidays.

Malaysian holidays begin in January through the Thaipusam celebration. This is when devotess celebrate at the Batu Caves, carrying offerings to show penance. Tourists flock the country during this time of the year to take part in the celebration. In February, Chinese New Year is celebrated not only in the country but in all other countries where there are Chinese people. From April to May, visitors can experience the Malaysia Water Festival where water-based activities are done. Participants take place in aquatic sports and a lot of water-sports enthusiasts and tourists visit the country.

Another celebration in May also takes part which attracts more visitors in the country. The Tadau Ka'amatan, celebrated from May 30 to 31, to give thanks to Bambaazon in Sabah. During the festival, food and rice wine are abundant and dancing on the streets is displayed. Another celebration on the same month is the Vesak where Buddhists give religious offerings and light their joss sticks. This is also the same time when monks are ordinated around the country.

By May to June, the Colors of Malaysia event starts with a beautiful, colorful parade showcasing the diverse culture of the peoples in the country. During the festival, people also dance on the streets and enjoy good music. In June, the Gawai, or the harvest festival is also celebrated through traditional ceremonies. Communal homes or long houses are venues for dancing around the state.

The Food and Fruit Fiesta is celebrated in the country in July. Tourists who want to enjoy good Malaysian cuisine and delicious foods in the country will surely enjoy this festival.

Crowd favorites include the nasi lemak and satay which are abundant fruit desserts during this month-long celebration. The festival is then followed by Malaysia's National Day celebrated on August 31. This is when the entire country remembers the Merdeka Day or their independence.

Malaysians also have their Lantern and Mooncake Festival happening during mid-autumn season. During this time, colorful lanterns are displayed while enjoying mooncakes. This festival is a celebration of peace and prosperity among the people in the country. In November, the Deepavali is celebrated with a display of lights adorning every home with oil lanterns. This is also done with a morning bathing ritual and spending time in prayers in temples. On the same month, the country celebrates the month of Ramadan. The end of the celebration, Han Raya Aidilfitni, special prayers are offered in mosques and visits to friends and relatives are also done. Sweet treats are also prepared and shared with fellow Muslims.

Although Malaysia is predominantly Muslim, there are also Christians in the country that attend church services. By December, Christians in the country celebrate Christmas where dinners and gifts are exchanged during this day.

See You In Malaysia!

After you've read our travel guide to Malaysia, we hope that your next vacation will be spent in the country. Take part of the diversified culture and experience the mouth-watering dishes served with authentic flavors. Dive in scuba diving sites and bring along with you souvenirs of great memories. Shop around the country and don't forget to take pictures with exotic animals found only in Malaysian. After the experience, you can now answer why Malaysia is Truly Asia!

Experience Everything Travel Guide Collection™

www.ingramcontent.com/pod-product-compliance
Lightning Source LLC
Chambersburg PA
CBHW071807020426
42331CB00008B/2422